love one another
the last days of jesus

retold by Lauren Thompson
illustrated by Elizabeth Uyehara

scholastic press ━ new york

for owen — L.T.

for walden
and charlotte — E.U.

Text copyright © 2000 by Lauren Thompson
Illustrations copyright © 2000 by Elizabeth Uyehara
All rights reserved. Published by Scholastic Press, a division of Scholastic Inc.,
Publishers since 1920. SCHOLASTIC and SCHOLASTIC PRESS and associated logos are
trademarks and/or registered trademarks of Scholastic Inc.

LIBRARY OF CONGRESS CATALOGING-IN-PUBLICATION DATA
Thompson, Lauren.
Love one another: the last days of Jesus / retold by Lauren Thompson; illustrated by Elizabeth Uyehara.   p. cm.
Summary: Recalls how Jesus taught people to love, how he was crucified for his teachings,
and how his resurrection brought hope to the world.

ISBN 0-590-31830-6

1. Jesus Christ — Resurrection — Juvenile literature. 2. Jesus Christ — Biography — Passion Week — Juvenile literature.
[1. Jesus Christ — Passion. 2. Jesus Christ — Resurrection. 3. Easter.]
I. Uyehara, Elizabeth, ill. II Title.   BT481.T515 2000   232.9'7 — dc21 99-25157   CIP

10 9 8 7 6 5 4 3 2 1   o/o 01 02 03 04

Printed in Singapore 46
First edition, March 2000

The text type was set in Matrix Extra Bold.
The display type was set in Democtratica Bold.
Book design by Marijka Kostiw

The paintings in this book were rendered in oil on canvas.

This retelling is drawn from the Gospels according to Matthew, Mark, Luke, and John
of the New Revised Standard Version of the Bible.

Special thanks to the Rev. Dr. W. Frederick Wooden, Senior Minister,
First Unitarian Church, Brooklyn, New York, for his expert advice.
For their enthusiastic and thoughtful support, the author also wishes to thank Charlotte Fleck
and the dedicated team of editors and designers who helped to bring this book about.

I was a young child when I first heard the story of Jesus's last days, his death and the miracle of Easter. Now that I am grown and have a child of my own, the story moves me even more powerfully. To me, whatever else the story may be, it is a human story that shows us at our best and our worst.

In Jesus we find a man who urges us to live simply and openly, trusting in God and in the power of love. He cares for the outcast and the downtrodden, people many of us turn away from. He teaches that as we forgive, so we will find forgiveness, and that above all we must love one another.

The figure of Jesus shows us who we could be. What happens to Jesus shows us who, too often, we really are. Most of the people around Jesus choose to act out of cowardice and hate rather than love. Even the disciples, who love him deeply, abandon him at his time of greatest need. Jesus's story reminds us how easy it is to choose fear over trust, and hate over love, and how awful the consequences can be.

But the story does not end there. In the midst of the disciples' terrible anguish, they come to understand at last the full meaning of Jesus's teachings of love and forgiveness. For though they have committed horrible wrongs against him, they feel he has forgiven them, and they are able to find peace. They are redeemed by the certainty that as long as Jesus's message of love lives on through them, then he has not truly died. The power of his teachings will be with them always, guiding their hearts toward peace and joy.

Thus the story of Jesus's last days is one of pain, but ultimately one of hope. The heart of the Easter miracle is this: No sorrow is so great that love cannot heal it. This is the message I wish to pass on to my son, and to all children, through this book.

— Lauren Thompson

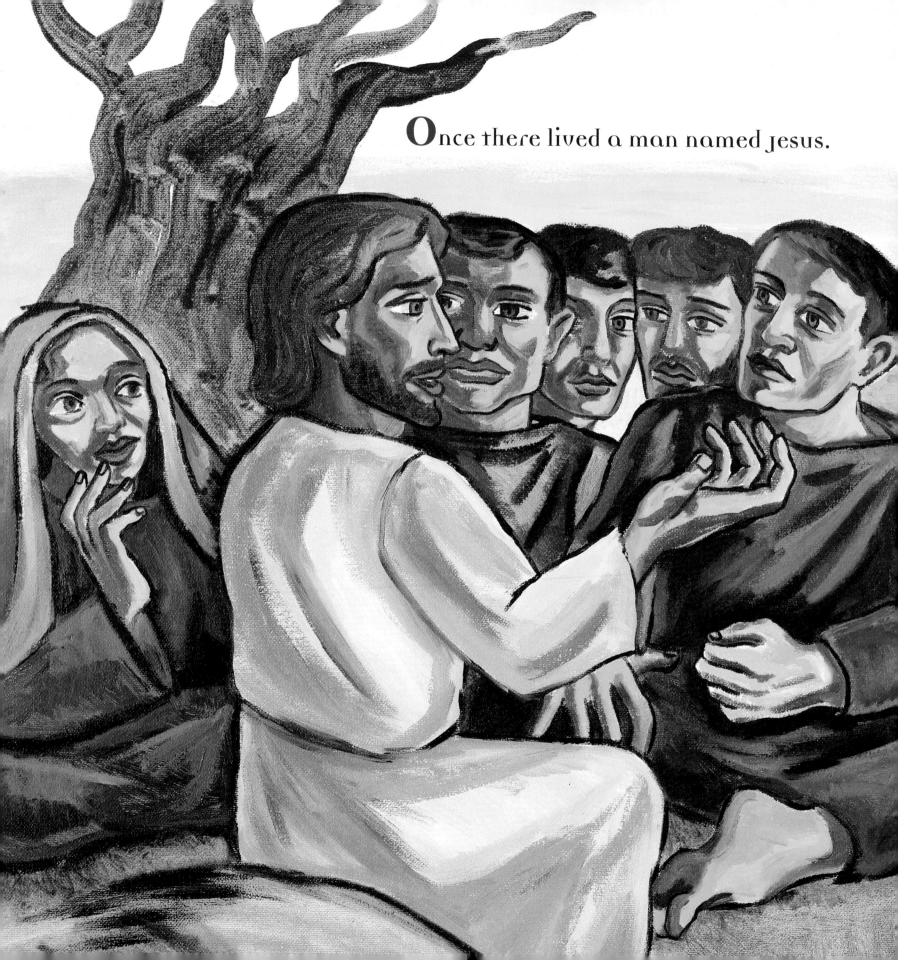

Once there lived a man named Jesus.

Jesus was a teacher. He was wise and good,
kind to the poor, the sick, and the outcast.
He traveled the countryside
and spoke to all of God's love and forgiveness.
Jesus taught, "Love your neighbor,
both friend and enemy,
for in heaven all are loved.
Forgive those who wrong you,
and you, too, will be forgiven.
Trust in God. And love one another."

Many who gathered to listen
were filled with hope and comfort.
Jesus taught, "God is always near.
Heaven is all around us even now.
We have only to look for it."

Some who heard Jesus's teachings
wanted to be with him always,
to learn his ways and wisdom.
They left all they had and became his disciples.
They did not always understand what Jesus taught,
but they loved him, as he loved them.

One day Jesus led his disciples
to the great city of Jerusalem.
When he entered the gates of the city,
people cheered as if he were a king.

Jesus went to the holy temple and began to teach,
and again he spoke of love.
A man asked, "Which of all teachings is greatest?"
Jesus answered, "Love God, and love one another.
These teachings together are the greatest."

Crowds drew near to hear
Jesus's simple but powerful words.
The temple priests grew angry with him, and envious.
"Does he think he is wiser than we are?"
they grumbled to one another.
"Does he think he is a new king?"

All week, as Jesus taught in the temple,
the priests plotted how to arrest him.

One evening, Jesus gathered his disciples
for a meal away from the crowds.
"I have wanted to be with you
one last time," Jesus said.
"For soon, I fear, one of you will betray me."
The disciples were saddened and alarmed.
They each asked, "Do you mean me?"
And they wondered which of them
could betray the teacher they loved.
They did not know that for thirty silver coins
the disciple named Judas had agreed
to help the priests arrest Jesus.

Later, Jesus and the disciples
went together to a garden.
Only Judas did not follow them.

Jesus was deeply grieved and troubled.
He knew that something terrible
would soon happen.
He asked his disciples to keep watch
while he prayed.
The disciples wanted to do as Jesus asked.
But they were weary and could not stay awake.
Full of sorrow, Jesus prayed alone.
"Whatever may come,
let God's will be done."

Jesus woke the disciples where they lay.
"Could you not keep watch for even one hour?"
he asked sadly.
"Rise, for the one who will betray me is here."
Just then, Judas entered the garden,
leading a band of soldiers sent by the priests.
Judas called to Jesus, "Teacher!"
And he kissed him.
Jesus whispered, "Friend, do what you have come to do."

Then the soldiers took hold of Jesus.
For the kiss had been a sign to seize him.
The soldiers led Jesus away,
but the disciples did not follow.
They were afraid they, too, would be captured.
They deserted Jesus and fled.

That night, the temple priests gathered
to judge their prisoner Jesus.
They questioned him and mocked him, asking,
"Do you not call yourself a king?"
Jesus answered only, "You say that I do."
For he knew the priests had already judged against him.
The priests grew even angrier.
They declared that Jesus had broken the holy laws
and should be punished with death.

At dawn, they brought Jesus to Pilate,
the Roman ruler of the land.
Pilate, too, questioned Jesus,
"Are you then a new king?"
Jesus answered only, "So you are saying."
Pilate could find no proof that Jesus had done wrong.
But the priests had stirred up the crowd outside.
"Put him to death!" they cried."Put him to death!"
Pilate feared the angry crowd.
He let the soldiers take Jesus away.

The soldiers brought Jesus to a hill outside the city, and they put him on a cross.

Jesus uttered a final prayer.

And then he died.

A man who loved Jesus took his body
and carefully placed it in a tomb.
He rolled a large stone in front of the opening.
Then he left to mourn the death of Jesus.

Two days later,
another friend of Jesus,
a woman named Mary,
came to the tomb.
The large stone had been rolled away.
Mary looked inside the dark opening.
The tomb was empty!

Mary began to cry.
She was afraid that someone
had taken Jesus's body.
Then she saw a man close by.
She heard him ask,
"Why are you crying?"
And she answered,
"Someone has taken our dear teacher away.
Can you tell me where?"
Then she heard the man call her by name:
"Mary!"
Suddenly she knew him.
It was Jesus she saw before her!
She heard him say,
"Go tell the others what you have seen."

Mary found the disciples
where they had gathered in hiding.
"Jesus lives!" she exclaimed.
But the disciples did not believe her.
They were deep in mourning,
weeping with grief and remorse.
For they knew they had deserted Jesus,
and then he had died.

Suddenly they saw Jesus there among them.
The disciples were startled and afraid.
"Do not be troubled," they heard Jesus say.
"Be at peace, and know that I am with you always."

Then the disciples rejoiced.
Their grief was ended.
For Jesus had died,
and yet he lived!

"Go, now," they heard Jesus say,
"teach others as I have taught you:
forgive and love.
As I have loved you,
so you must love one another."

The disciples were filled with
great peace and happiness.
For now they understood in their hearts
what Jesus had taught.
They knew their wrongs were forgiven
and that love was greater than hate,
greater even than death.
In his love, Jesus lived on.

Joyously the disciples set out
to bring Jesus's teachings to everyone,
and to tell the wondrous story of this day,
Easter Day,
to all the world.